Tapestry of Silence

Lokareddy Prishitha Reddy

BookLeaf Publishing

India | USA | UK

Presentation by *BookLeaf Publishing*

Web: www.bookleafpub.com

E-mail: info@bookleafpub.com

ISBN: 9789363318267

First edition 2024

"To courage,

I offer my deepest gratitude,

for enduring my tears and insecurities."

PREFACE

Patience, once treasured, now fades amidst emotional voyages. As I type these words (like a typewriter), sadness quietly treads. My journey into poetry began during my Bachelor's, where "Dalgona coffee was our companion."

I proudly present my debut poetry collection, "Tapestry of Silence." As your fingers gracefully turn each page with your beautiful palm, you'll embark on an emotional journey, welcomed by my dear friends, Nervous and Anxious. Here, I tenderly offer my poetic baby to you.

PS: I do the official overthinking through
Instagram: alrightypri
Handle with care,
An Overthinker,
Prishitha

Childhood

Childhood —
The most memorable time, they say,
The most beautiful and precious moments
which can't ever be discarded,
The blissfulness in that innocence is so pure
that the word 'confusion' is just an illusion!

Childhood —
The joy of doing immature things,
The joy of exploring unknown things,
The joy of Dad's special takeout treats,
The road was so clear
Until
We aged to adulting,
Where are you, dear joy?
Where are you, *"maduramaina"* childhood?
(*maduramaina* - sweet in English)
Why are you hiding somewhere
causing the 'I' to be in stress,
The 'WH' never wants to end
It's the purpose of life!

Childhood —
The innocence blossomed in young minds —
Playing with mud,

Playing in the school park,
Waiting for the sports hour to welcome
to play freely with hearts being light,
It's been the best days or moments!

Childhood —
Will it ever be back?
Will we ever have the time like those as of now?
Will the memories be enough like in the film
clips?

In Quiet Moments

His words and her smile
Believing that both care for each other
When they are reticent —
All they barely give a smile
that their heart wants to whisper something.

I wonder,
Are fairytales real?
Are we just gasping?
Believing that all are just glowing
in a parallel way
Those laughs, misunderstandings,
circumstances, and you reminiscing
about them,
All are but just the past, ahh!

Standing in awe on the veranda
Watching people how they're lively,
Pushing the boundaries of mine
To inculcate what I admire,
To just smile
And let the worries drown in the ocean!
Millions of people in the world
who dream to achieve
what they long for —

striving hard to be one in a million
of being comfortable and self-satisfied!

In the quiet moments,
I see the purpose of me
I see the abilities in me
I see all the things I wish for
But then, it vanishes away like the dread plants!

The Park

Stepping in the path of you
Flashes of you incoming,
The hope that rose —
a welcoming game
into the darkness of fears.

Stepping in the path of you
Walking in the park,
reflecting upon that —
It's not easy to make *'thoughts of you'* vanish
but not too difficult either,
Seeing people merely exercising in the park,
Watching the mothers and fathers letting their
children play,
Letting them fall and rise,
Letting them be *'themselves,'*
The father chasing after
her daughter in the park
making sure she is enjoying
what she's doing while also
helping her stay fit is so endearing!

Amidst all the work and timid tiredness,
taking a break from their routines
Relaxing in the nature they chose;

People just chatting—
As in grandmothers gossiping…
Sharing how their day went
And getting what they need most — relaxation!

The park has the power of amusements to
reinforce relaxation and peace in one's mind,
How can people not go and sit in the
shade of the tree and feel its warmth,
How can people not go and take the
blessings of trees and exchange smiles
with a fully reflex angle?

Stepping in the path of you
I might have lost these beautiful feelings,
Momentarily, I find amusement in myself
by letting you go,
gazing at the park's ethics,
with the library nestled within
brings me pure joy.

The City

The city is so vague
Full of memories,
People maintaining their socio-economic life,
People weekending,
People are either being biased or chauvinistic,
People going above and beyond.

The city is so vague
Built up with the stories
we have been learning since childhood,
Every place embraces the emotions
that go straight into the heart,
I'm in love with the blueness of the city
while thinking of green
that mesmerizes the beauty of the city,
and the shade of purple isn't likable
by the city, as humans
are twisted in their form,
who are possessed by trust and loyalty
which is sweet, yet the city
is grasped by the air of mystery.

The city is so vague
Doubtful in one's heart,
Doubtful of the verse –

the city wants us to be
Scattered and all alone!
Happiness is gray in the
world of confidence and competition,
Life here is a mist of ice and snow
where we are in an assumption
of being cold but indeed,
It's a crystalline delight.

The city is so vague
Scared of the response I give,
Scared of how it encapsulates,
Scared of so much and many things
But
It's you —
You would be ready to deal
with your inner fears,
to be gray in the world of yellow.

The city is so vague
Yet so determined and powerful.
Necessities, youthfulness,
and pleasure makes it cheerful,
You or we or us can't make everyone happy
But
evolve oneself in this city as a reverence.

Promises

Are promises even real?
Promises often turn into ashes,
The promise is no less than an apocalypse.
Today's era has been tremendous
Using emojis is not my thing —
My vocabulary had taken a fall
My investments in writing are tarnished
by the loan of the words over time,
I simply wanted to convey
I have zero knowledge of writing,
I have been failing in writing exams,
I'm full of disgrace and impotent
I hate how I have to do hard work!
Luck doesn't even look back once
As per the luck-based priority like investing,
My investments in writing are disgraced
by the loan of the words over time.

Are promises even real?
Promises turn into ashes
The promise is no less than an apocalypse.
I can't persuade you whether
I'm a good person or bad —
I'm just a person with mood swings
where my mamma and dada

call me *"confused"* with love,
where my friends describe me ultimately the
same,
Hence, I'm growing into a confused person,
more like I'm a contradiction of myself.

Are promises even real?
Promises turn into ashes
The promise is no less than an apocalypse.
What's my true self as a person?
What's it like to be just invested in me?
What's it like to be active?
Oopsie daisy! I can't stick
at some point, I simply declare defeat!

Moments infuriating me hard,
Fear awakening in me now and then
Tears invoking me usually at night,
Fictional characters make me smile (hehee)!
Home sometimes feels 'boring'
And
Just my mind is overwhelmed,
caught between load and brakes,
Soul and mind are so busy
having a conversation
Yet I feel empty that I'm
not supposed to be loved and cared for.

Embrace I —

What's it to touch yourself?
What's akin to skin embracing?
What's so special that it hurts?
What's so special is that it keeps you warm —
What's that when touched, makes you hug
yourself?

If it's not the skin we embrace —
If it's not about the skin we spend eternity
If it's just about the part we forget that
it's the perceptiveness of our life,
Then what could it possibly be?

Embracing the skin,
Embracing the beauty,
Embracing and touching,
A sensation is that one can
feel, other than you —
Ahhh! Skin, I'm in awe of you.
I'm wholly in awe of you —
For making me believe in myself,
For making me feel safe,
For turning into the person I can't ever be,
For also giving me acne — why? (a small
giggle)

I can't let the particles of you vanish
But
Let's promise that we'll abide by each other.

Embracing my skin is the
least I've ever done,
I was a dead plant with thorns
who just swayed in the field,
Not knowing the area
can always be the same.

Embrace, embrace, embrace
It's yours, not others!
Embrace, embrace, embrace
Even if it's painful too!
Embrace, embrace, embrace
'Cause it's all of us —
Give a hug
You'll embrace it like never before.

Beauty and Who

Beauty and the beast never go hand in hand
Beauty lies in its way
It's a philosophy!

Beauty and the beast never go hand in hand
Its ugliness and emptiness share intrusive
thoughts
It's a reality!

Beauty and the beast never go hand in hand
Beast dances to its own laws' tune
It's so harsh!

Beauty and the beast never go hand in hand
What if the fierce creature once neglected is now
a tender soul?
The beast transformed into a darling,
while intelligence reigns
as the epitome of beauty.

Beauty and the beast — a paradoxical pair
Like lines of my poetry,
buried beneath the soul,
Not to embellish
but beauty eludes definition.

Yet the beast roars,
the life of the celestial soirée!

14

The Stare

Millions of miles I walk a day
Staring at the book,
For millions of days,
I long for the characters
of the book to vince,
Headsets bearing me —
books are resting,
As I tilt my face up, I see
the "ones" STARING at me
from head to foot,
The scary thought seems to be
"I'm on my own now."

Millions of stare I get err' day
The anxiety in me rises,
Being in therapy in the nick of time
was the best decision I made,
The hindrance, ahh —
Getting better err' twenty-four/seven,
Giving myself a hand —
A magical moment that's inexplicable.

For millions of ages (uhhh-ahh)
I hid from you
Not knowing you, 'the stare'

could be agonizing,
In the stillness of the night
my world begins to take flight,
The allocation of my world
makes a step through 'eyeing'
and smiling at them,
To my astonishment,
few smile back at me
While the others make faces.

Millions of miles I walk a day
Millions of stare I get err' day
For millions of ages (eehh)
I hid from you
But
I don't need to fill in for someone, instead
I'm making room for the dreams I desire.

If I Ever Write a Song

If I ever write a song —
How would that be?
What would that be?
Will my soul be at rest?

If I ever write a song
My insecurities would rise high to a tremor
My happiness would take the last place
My tremor beholds me as always.

If I ever write a song
It mightn't be on you
'Cause all I just get is a question!
'Cause all of it makes me think of —
"Why does the world always keep on judging
another set of humans who are enjoying
their space ohhhhhh?"

If I ever write a song
The trees merely give me a hug,
The clouds make me smile,
The sun has always been in
a hate-love relationship with me.

If I ever write a song

The lyrics would be dancing
in the happiness of its tune,
as they knew their meaning would
bring smiles to the people.

If I ever write a song
The compassion in me
would metaphorize the world,
Instill the loneliness in me,
Making me see the world through
my perception,
the realization of the old to
the new me is enraged..

If I ever write a song
I don't know if this would be a to-do list
But I know I'll be the happiest
As I'm experimenting with the experience of a
bitter-sweet life.

If I ever write a song
I don't know how my family
and friends would react,
I don't know whether their reaction
would make me feel like a wet weekend
or bring a grin from ear to ear,
Would they be proud of me, oh oh oh?

If I ever write a song about myself

How would it be?
What would it be?
I doubt whether it'd make my soul rest.

Silent Verse

I'm not a great writer
Nor can I ever be,
The words in my dictionary
Seem to throw pebbles at me
For not being intriguing.

I'm not a great writer
Nor can I ever be,
My words fall weak
In front of the greatest poets;
I'll be flustered while communicating
with the people;
I'm no less than a disaster,
When it's time to unleash my talent.

I'm not a great writer
Nor can I ever be,
I'm just an open book
To the ones who understand
And I'm a closed door
to those who treat me like a mistake.

I'm not a great writer
Nor can I ever be,
The paths are yet to be discovered

The fear in me has profoundly deepened
And I feel dumb and numb.

I'm not a great writer
Nor can I ever be,
OR
Will I ever be?
Or
Is it just the offshore
Tryin' to inculcate the onshore moments?

I'm not a great writer
Nor can I ever be!

Memories

How do I really define the phrase
"MEMORIES?"
How do I know if I'm still a part of them?
How do I understand if my soul was acting in
the life of this phrase?
How do I know why and when I answer, but
"BUT" never listened?

How do I redefine the phrase *"MEMORIES"*?
Is it the first meetings or the
ends that didn't cross the path?
Is it the first shared laughs or
last unspoken words?
Is it the secrets beholding or
being a bad secret keeper?
Is it the hugs that keep you warm or
the *"people"* who harbor hate?

How do I redefine the phrase *"MEMORIES"*?
Was it visiting *"Ammamma's"* place during
holidays?
Was it going on a family trip to relieve stress?
Was it back in the *"past ol' days,"* the good
one?
Was that not being nurturing unknown?

How do I redefine the phrase *"MEMORIES"*?
Will I ever be able to?
Would I like the past ol' days
more than the present, which feels scary?
What if *"being in the present"* is something I
hate more than I enjoyed the past?
Perhaps I couldn't define the memories as it's
uncertain
    To be replenished as the present.

I - Bitter or Sweet

I — just a letter that misleads me with many
thoughts
I — not just me, but all the people who revolve
around us
I is someone whose perspective is least
considered,
I — the version has been updated
The version before and the version now are
rivals!

I, where have you been?
I, what's your paradigm of yourself?
I, have been digging in abundance lately!
I, have a shelter to rent on
    there's always a *'but'* to make things worse!

I, what's going on?
I,
  I,
    I,
      I,
        I,
          I…… just won't be in the stop phase
'Cause humans are called *'Curious people'*

I, in a deeply thoughtful state, screamed —
  "Tell me I'm fine
   Tell me I'm not so mad
   Tell me I could be nice.
   Tell me this is not what it was meant to be,
   Tell me we're good
   Tell me the world gets nicer soon
   Tell me I'm not broke
   Tell me I'm not weak
   Tell me, the diary of my pages is just the
beginning….."

Screaming doesn't end,
Manifestation won't stop dreaming,
Curiosity turns into apathy,
The blood starts to boil from the tip of the
fingers
      that's the pain of anguish!
As Taylor Swift said
"YOU'RE ON YOUR OWN KID"
   Either you'll fail or be happy,
   everything is on you.
Let the light fall in the FALL OF 'Canopy'!

The Nightmare

A dream that's wide and open
A dream that's been embedded in me
A dream that gasps for air
A dream that tempts relentlessly
A dream that's been built
What is it in reality that shatters me?

A dream where I imagined
the floor was full of blood stains,
Zombies and witches glaring at each other,
The devastation had been enraging in me.

My mind is spinning like a whirlpool —
The insanity is distorts past reality,
The lies and truths have been twisted.
As I open my eyes,
The blood is on my abdomen and hands.

A dream that's wide and open
It's been damaging my brain for a month.
Blood and stains appear everywhere I step,
It's been appearing and disappearing
Trapped in a loop.

A dream that's wide and open

It has encapsulated me,
Enveloped in tremors,
Dismay with disgust of dreadfulness.
After a week,
I could finally breathe,
Confronted by the series of visions that
Have deeply intrigued something in me!

Anxiety

Quieter yet scared,
Lighter yet heavier,
Negative yet not positive,
Cheeks glowing (not really),
Cheeks in sorrow,
While JOY is unwelcomed.

Quieter yet scared,
Lighter yet heavier,
A subdued sound: *"tap, tap, tap"* —
The light shone to dark
Unsudden gasped moment it was,
Step by step, path by path
sweat rolling down to cheeks,
Hands folded, silence ingrained.

Quieter yet scared,
Lighter yet heavier,
Silence flows through the ears.
The *"tap, tap, tap"* astonishingly instills fear
as the soul is separating from my body,
Burden and the heart are being rivals,
The sound coming from the door,
Darkness being the transformation —
Senses like someone throwing me into the pool.

Quieter yet scared,
Lighter yet heavier,
Eyes closed followed by a twitch,
a scream escapes
Realized it was when ANXIETY was born.

Illusions Unraveled

As I step forward
I could sense the spontaneity consumed,
As I step backward
I could feel the time slipping away,
As I step forward with eyes open in the dark
I, I, I…
could feel the 'alarm' in the way
the clock had shut down my soul.
Is it an illusion?

I feel trapped ….
Enclosed within a hollow sphere
I feel I couldn't get out of '8' —
    Stuck in a cycle where it never ends.
I still hope to shine
But
I'm rinsed to the core of *"I hate it here"*
Is it an illusion?

I'm lonely…..
I'm too lonely and wandering
aaaaaaaaaaaauhhhh
Wandering silently in the labyrinth of dreams,
I'm not so fearsome, rather I exaggerate,
Yet I'm in my youthful years

I sensate the weight of age and
How it whispers *"I hate it here"*
Is it an illusion?

I'm too crooked to even have a taught thought
It's bitter and funny how I wrote these lines
as I'm worthless to write them
and to consider myself as a poet,
Cause the only thing that dances in my mind is
  "Like a poet
  Trapped in someone's mind
  I hate it here
  My feelings don't depict
  as my words utter,
 Like a poet
In "my" era
Astounded and Sounded,
I hate it here…"
Secretly I want to dive into the
books of coffee shops,
Study literature, the humans
Because someone said it was fun.
(it would take a decade, with many hardships
among them)
And I'm struck here on the path of the ocean
where the waves are too tidal
And my journey isn't too easy,
I would die and be reborn
'Cause I'm a precocious child,

Is it all an illusion?

Is it all an illusion?
I woke up from the reality of reading a novel,
It's 9 a.m.
Couldn't unfold the mystery
Because everything had been an ILLUSION!

Devastation

My mouth is called *"Devastation"*
To realize that's danger —
It took me countless years!
The lost feature had already taken place
Being unknown was my source
Developing extroversion
    became a sharp angle,
Its retracting feature turned into introversion.

My mouth is called *"Devastation"*
Messing up was the mouth's ultimate work
Caught between speaking up or remaining silent
Immersed like a fish in a bowl
   Contemplating whether to drown or to be still.

My mouth is called *"Devastation"*
Unbreakable bonds made to *"Forever torn
apart"*
Self-blaming for an interpretation of one's
character
Losing the ones I care about
Once they were memories,
now they are wounds.

My mouth is called *"Devastation,"*

Uttering words that hurt people,
Learning to not be harmful,
Amending to harmony
By bidding adieu to devastation.

Love and Mindscapes

You blow up my mind
like clouds in the sky,
You blow up my mind
like no one ever has,
Is this something new
I have been feeling it lately, ohh?
knowing that I can't be anyone!
You blow up my mind
like trees swaying in the wind.

I see you holding a pack of cigars
I just want to stop you, ohh,
When I asked you, you said
"It gives me peace
It relieves the stress in me
I don't know how and why
all of a sudden
it gives me a heaven of happiness,
How could I let that go?
That doesn't mean I didn't
try to stop
But I wasn't able to back off,

All of this is me
And all of this is me,

If you want to be with me as I am,
I'll plant you in my heart forever."

Nevertheless, I can't abandon him,
His care and words struck me
He has blown up my mind
in every part of me.

She, with her patiently accepting eyes, said to
him,
"I'm ready to be involved in your soul
Internally, she whispers to herself —
Embracing you with love that binds,
Though I may not sway your stubborn mind,
One day, I'll claim your heart is divine.
With my love, I'll gently guide you,
Letting all your burdens drift away.
Our hands entwined, we smile
finding solace in each other's warmth.
*"Let's embody eternal love
and intertwine our souls forever."*

Beyond the Horizon's call

I always believed moving away from home
was all I needed, as beneath, I was an escapist,
Escapist IN EVERY WAY,
When I was twenty,
my tremor turned into poems
of documents that the words
overflowed in praising me.
As I neared the age of 22,
I so delved into publishing,
a pile of poems
crafted in a book
BUT
courage took a step back.

Journeying home away from home
was quite a different emotion,
Tremor, my unyielding companion clung to me.
Found beautiful mates —
    Adored and respected (really!?)
     as I'd never imagined,
(a short pause)
If everything's good
    WHY WOULD 'I' EVER EXIST?

I always believed moving away from home
was all I needed,
As said by Albert Einstein
 "Out of Chaos, find simplicity" —
I'm still chasing that simplicity
But all I could see is that I have painted
enough mess in the hearts I've broken.
I realized I can't always control my words,
Everything fell apart in the blink of an eye.
If I'd known I'd become this person,
    I wouldn't want to exist.

I always believed moving away from home
was all I needed,
I thought the insecurity I possessed left me,
But it still hurts and seems to scare me.
Bathroom floor cries have ended, hooray
(don't be too happy dear writer [evil face])
In the midst of laughter and joy,
Amidst cousins' cheerful play,
I cried in the bathroom
without letting out a sound outward as
I was a waste of material with zero
tolerance and patience,
I called myself dumb
but I hope not to be.
Another week, another day —
Quiet tears unspoken

Feeling like rain on a sunny day,
Inside a storm had taken place —
A storm of doubts and fears,
Yet masked and concealed.

I always believed moving away from home
was all I needed,
I was an ESCAPIST.
I still don't know what I'm doing
At twenty-three, I know *(or need to)*
I will get through it by moving forward,

All I want is to not lift the horizon's call beyond.

The Universe

The sun rises down
On the hope of emerging again the subsequent
day
But uhh-ohhh jealousy incoming —
The moon would be inheriting its position
By snatching the sun's warmth from its children!

The sun rises down
Knowing that the moon will rule at night,
But here comes the bliss —
Sun retracing, knowing the moon
will be taking care of their child,
showering it with love and care!

The sun rises down
Long naps happening
Plotting has been conspiring due to
the rivalry of day and night,
Engulfed in temper and anger of being
possessive for their child!

The sun and the moon
turned from enemies to friends
just to make their child happy,
But

The universe won't let them —
As the universe whispers in frustration
"I'm your leader and I have made a few rules
which this whole eternity should follow".

The sun and moon are the
life-givers of the universe.
There are lovers who can adjust to….
Could be lovers who converse endlessly,
It could be umm, most like the literature lovers
like Romeo-Juliet, Elizabeth Bennett-Darcy!

But my beautiful universe lovers —
"Sun and moon are made to
choose not to see each other
But they are eternity lovers
for their entire existence".

Bookish Souls

I dream of it often —
I see how smoothly the water runs in the ocean,
I see how they clasp hands while walking,
I see how beautifully they gaze at each other,
I see-saw as the water runs deep,
Yet the deep is too far from reality.

I dream of it often —
We are known as *"book girlies,"*
We read to hide from reality,
We are in awe of fictional loves,
Yes, we exist!
We chose Damon over Stefan
(haha, I do sometimes).
As the water runs deep,
the quiet depth brings tranquility.

I dream of it, umm...
Whenever my fingers turn pages,
The emotions in me swell with curiosity.
Imaginary lines bestow butterflies,
We laugh, we cry, we hate, and love —
we become emotional fools
yet we endure every moment.
In coffee shops, with bookmarks placed,

sounds become silent verse,
Engagement becomes poetry.
As the water runs deep,
We raise our bars until they sink.

I dream of it—
the vast chasm from reel to real.
Novels are part of our journey,
Each word echoes a moment's phase,
from crushing on *"Atlas Corrigan"*
or *"Ryle Kincaid"* to
envisioning *"Adam Connor,"* my soul dances.
We, the book girlies, imagine
floods rising deep in our hearts.
We, as book girlies, feel
deeply for our fictional loves.
We, as book girlies,
nurture every detail.
In libraries or cozy beds,
Books are our pillows,
words, our threads.
They weave our thoughts in stories' grace,
Finding magic in every place.

As a child, tales were told,
As a teen, novel exploration began,
Now as an adult, lessons have been
learned of love and heartbreak.
In highs and lows, books

remain steadfast companions.
As the water runs deep,
the heart winds like the secret rivers.

Threads of Silence

*"But how could you live and have no story to
tell?"*
A quote from Fyodor Dostoevsky's *White Nights*
intrigued me to reflect on life's perspective.

I'm just a girl who fantasies about poetry,
Basically the opposition of dreaming —
    (Yeah, you're right! In reality)
Might be a girl who's a struggler
with clarity and being impotent.

I'm just a girl who's enchanted
by the nature of kindness,
I'm just a girl who's naive and equally dumb.
I'm just a girl who's aiming to be a lady/woman
But often stumbles by being an immature girl.

I'm just a girl who reigns on
the throne of her happiness,
I'm just a girl who apologizes to a
Inanimate things if they're hurt by 'I'
I'm just a girl where poetry
give birth to her soul —
        finds home in BOOKS,
I'm just a girl who does her

best for success but failure seizes.

I'm just a girl who intends to be perfect
but always ends up as an idiot,
I'm just a girl in the stillness of the
library amidst whispered words,
    she musters the strength to be courageous.
I'm just a girl —
whose stories are untold,
Every day is the
beginning of a karmic presence
and each emotion ignites lines of poetry,
of a girl who weaves her own narrative.

I'm just a girl —
who's not proud of herself,
whose emotions have been blocked,
Seeking imprisonment from *"the blockness."*

In awe of Tapestry of Silence
Bottling up the bitter or sweet
with memories being devastated
and promises to be a novice.

In the era of Tapestry of Silence
I chose to be a silencer
by gazing through the window
how beautiful the world is
Yet striving for impeccability.

www.ingramcontent.com/pod-product-compliance
Lightning Source LLC
Chambersburg PA
CBHW072049150726
47996CB00015B/2461